BIRMINGHAM
IN THE
THIRTIES

Alton & Jo Douglas

Snow Hill Station, Colmore Row, 13th October 1938.

© 2002 Alton and Jo Douglas
ISBN 1 85858 214 8
Published by Brewin Books Ltd., Doric House, 56 Alcester Road, Studley, Warwickshire B80 7LG.
Printed by Warwick Printing Co. Ltd., Theatre Street, Warwick CV34 4DR.
Layout by Alton and Jo Douglas

A hold-up, due to a pre-war blackout rehearsal, Martineau Street, 4th November 1938.

Front Cover: Rea Street/High Street, Deritend, May 1934.

Contents

BREWIN BOOKS LTD

Doric House, 56 Alcester Road,
Studley, Warwickshire B80 7LG

Tel: 01527 854228 Fax: 01527 852746

Vat Registration No. 705 0077 73

Dear Nostalgic,

Have you ever stopped to think what a decade the thirties was for architectural exits and entrances? A great many "stately homes" (Granges, Halls, Houses, etc.) disappeared and a whole host of "palaces" (of the picture variety) made their debut. Despite the depression and, almost as if in obstinate anticipation of today's informal ways, people went out of their way to dress up to relax – if you want to see a wonderful array of collars and ties just look at photographs of men on the beach and in the park! It may also come as a surprise to see that, as early as 1936, there were quite extensive preparations for a possible war.

As you set off on your exploratory voyage bear in mind that we've tried to create the illusion that all of thirties life is represented here. For a while lose today and become a part of the past.

Yours, in friendship,

Alton

Singers Hill Synagogue, Blucher Street, 4th April 1939.

Hob Moor Ford, Hay Mills, 1930.

Edward Road Baptist Church Hockey Team, Balsall Heath, 1930.

Machine Shop B, Austin Motor Co. Ltd., Longbridge Works,
Longbridge, c. 1930.

Bull Ring, 1930.

Old Square/Corporation Street, c. 1930.

The official opening ceremony of the impressive Central Avenue wrought-iron gates, University of Birmingham, May 1930.

Old Inn, Cannon Hill Park, 1930.

Lozells Street Junior School, c. 1930.

Northfield C of E School, Church Hill, 1930.

Bournville Station, 1930.

Parties arriving for conducted tours around Cadbury's Bournville Lane, Summer 1930.

Once a week, during the lunch hour, the girls enjoy an open air concert, Cadbury's, Summer 1930.

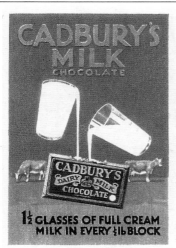

Showing the food value of Milk Chocolate.

Heralding the now famous "Sandwich Block."

Telling in an attractive way that Bournville products (which are articles of food, are "Made in Ideal Conditions."

The finest value in the shops!

If you spend 2d. on a block of Bournville plain chocolate you know you are getting chocolate of Cadbury quality. Its flavour is assured by Cadburys insistence upon the Empire's choicest cocoa beans ; its velvety smoothness is assured by Cadburys wealth of experience and skill. That's why Bournville is the finest plain chocolate. You also know how much chocolate you are getting : 2 ozs. net—checked and guaranteed.

What better value can your 2d. buy?

CADBURYS

Northfield Cinema, Bristol Road South, 1930.

The Odeon, just prior to opening, Perry Barr, August 1930. It had the distinction of being the first Odeon in the country.

Hazelwell Football Club's combined teams, Stirchley, 1930.

Jack Payne and his Band, Birmingham Hippodrome, August 1930.

Celebrating the jubilee of the opening of Mason College,
with Lady Astor surrounded by dignitaries, Edmund Street,
October 1930.

H.G. Shakespeare, Raddlebarn Road, Selly Oak, 1931.

JAMES Wm GLOVER & SONS, LTD.
10, DIGBETH, BIRMINGHAM,
Warwick and Bridge Foot, Stratford-on-Avon,

HAVE pleasure in thanking you for your kind remittance, and enclose receipt herewith. They very much appreciate the business you have entrusted to them, and hope to be favoured with your further esteemed orders, which will always have their best attention.

Your kind recommendation will also be appreciated.

Ernest Burton outside his shop in Oxhill Road, Handsworth, 1931.

Class 7, St John's C of E School, Johnstone Street, Ladywood, 1931. The boy in the centre of the back row is Alton's uncle, the author, Victor J. Price.

Kings Norton Church and the Old Grammar School,
The Green, 1931.

Bristol Road, near Witherford Way, Selly Oak, June 1931.

Greenwood Avenue, Hall Green, 15th June 1931.

A new bus, ready for service on the Acocks Green route, 1931.

Balsall Heath Road, 1931.

The Friends' Meeting House, Bull Street, 30th June 1931. The last meeting for worship had just been held and the building was awaiting demolition to make way for a new meeting house almost on the same spot.

Middlemore Road/West Heath Road, Northfield, 1931.

Middlemore Road, Northfield, 1931.

General Post Office, Victoria Square/Hill Street, October 1931.

Visiting day in the main control room of Nechells Power Station, 1st October 1931.

Bull Street, looking towards High Street,
14th December 1931.

PRINCIPAL EVENTS OF 1931

JAN. 3. Death of Marshal Joseph Jacques Césaire Joffre, French soldier.

,, 4. Death of the Princess Royal—Princess Louise, the King's eldest sister.

,, 16. The Prince of Wales accompanied by Prince George left London for Paris by air on the first stage of their tour to South Africa.

,, 19. India Round Table Conference ends.

,, 22. Death of Anna Pavlova.

,, 29. In an explosion at the Whitehaven Colliery, 26 men lost their lives.

FEB. 3. Earthquake in New Zealand. Town of Napier destroyed.

,, 4. Lady Houston's guarantee of £100,000 for Schneider Trophy.

,, 5. Malcolm Campbell breaks world's motor speed record at 246 m.p.h. at Daytona.

,, 10. Viceroy Lord Irwin inaugurates New Delhi as capital of India.

,, 19. Mrs. Victor Bruce arrives at Lympne after world flight.

,, 21. Malcolm Campbell knighted.

,, 23. Death of Dame Nellie Melba.

,, 28. Sir Oswald Mosley forms new party.

MAR. 21. Cambridge won the Boat Race, their 8th successive victory.

,, 22. "Royal Scot" train wrecked near Leighton Buzzard; 6 deaths.

,, 26. Death of Timothy Michael Healy, first Governor-General of the Irish Free State.

,, 27. Death of Arnold Bennett; novelist and dramatist.

APR. 2. Kay Don breaks world's motor boat speed record, reaching 103.49 miles an hour.

,, 4. First official air mail for Australia leaves Croydon.

,, 6. Glen Kidston reaches Capetown after record flight of 6½ days.

,, 10. C. W. A. Scott creates record by flying to Australia in 9 days, 4 hours, 11 minutes.

,, 14. Abdication of King Alphonso of Spain.

,, 26. Census taken.

MAY 14. First air mail from Australia.

,, 22. Whipsnade Zoo opened.

,, 27. Professor Piccard ascends nearly 10 miles in balloon.

JUNE 3. Derby won by Mr. J. A. Dewar's Cameronian.

,, 5. C. W. A. Scott makes record flight from Australia to Lympne (10 days, 13 hours).

,, 9. British submarine, *Poseidon*, sunk off Wei-hai-Wei; 20 lives lost.

JULY 10. King opens George V dock at Glasgow.

,, 27. Death of Viscount Knutsford.

AUG. 6. J. A. Mollison beats C. W. A. Scott's record in flight from Australia to England. Time 8 days 22 hrs. 25 min.

,, 18. Graf Zeppelin flew from Friedrichshafen to London and toured over England.

,, 23. Labour Government resigns.

,, 24. Mr. Ramsay MacDonald forms National Government.

,, 31. Death of Sir Thomas Henry Hall Caine; novelist.

SEPT. 13. Britain finally wins Schneider Trophy; third consecutive victory.

,, 14. "Cheltenham Flyer" establishes record for fastest train, 78 m.p.h.

,, 21. Britain off Gold Standard.

,, 29. Fl.-Lt. G. H. Stainforth makes world air speed record 408.8 m.p.h.

,, 29. Death of Sir William Orpen; British artist.

OCT. 2. Death of Sir Thomas Lipton, merchant and yachtsman.

,, 8. Lord Trenchard appointed Commissioner of the Police of the Metropolis in succession to Viscount Byng, who resigned.

,, 18. Death of Thomas Alva Edison, world-famous inventor.

,, 27. General Election: Majority for National Government.

NOV. 5. Miss Peggy Salaman and Mr. Gordon Store complete new record flight to the Cape (5 days, 6 hours, 40 minutes).

,, 9. A. C. Butler sets up new record in flight from England to Port Darwin (9 days, 2 hours, 29 minutes).

DEC. 10. Nobel Peace Prize for 1931 divided between Miss Jane Addams and Dr. Nicholas Murray Butler.

,, 30. Mr. Fielder, a British air pilot, flew from London to Algiers in a day.

1932

St. James's Church, Barrack Street, Duddeston, 1932.

Class 4c, Handsworth Grammar School, Grove Lane, 1932.

APPEAL for £90,000

The General Hospital	. . .	£50,000
The Queen's Hospital	. . .	£30,000
The Ear and Throat Hospital		£10,000

These amounts are urgently needed to prevent closing of beds and to enable the three Hospitals to continue their full service to the City and surrounding districts.

The dress rehearsal of "Street Scene", Repertory Theatre, Station Street, 28th January 1932.

Donald Garth Brown outside Brown's confectionery shop, Jakeman Road, Balsall Heath, c. 1932.

MIDLAND AMATEUR TITLES.

B. TUCKER AGAIN QUALIFIES TO MEET F. EDWARDS. 30/1/32

The Midland Amateur Championships were proceeded with at the Castle Hotel, Birmingham, when in the semi-final of the billiards event B. Tucker (Birmingham) beat L. Rouse (Birmingham) by 356 points. Thus he qualified, as last season, to oppose F. Edwards (Stourbridge) in the final, which will take place on Monday evening. Tucker played very soundly, and twice came within range of the century, making breaks of 78 and 80, besides 32 (twice), 46, 26, 27 and 25. Rouse's only break of note was 35. Result: Tucker 500, Rouse 144.

In the first round of the snooker championship J. H. Cooper (Birmingham) beat W. Tirebuck (Birmingham) by three games to two. Tirebuck won the first by 61—12, but Cooper, however, played a clever safety game in the second and third to win by 54—29 and 63—17. Tirebuck levelled matters by winning the fourth by 53—44, Cooper missing an easy pink. Cooper won the decider by 77—27.

Dingley's Hotel, Moor Street, c. 1932.

A village pump still in use in Yardley, March 1932.

Chamberlain Place, 7th March 1932.

Fred Perry takes part in the Tally Ho tournament, Edgbaston, 29th March 1932. Three years later he became the Wimbledon singles champion.

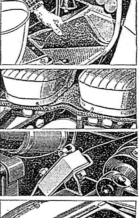

Garrison Lane, Bordesley, c. 1932.

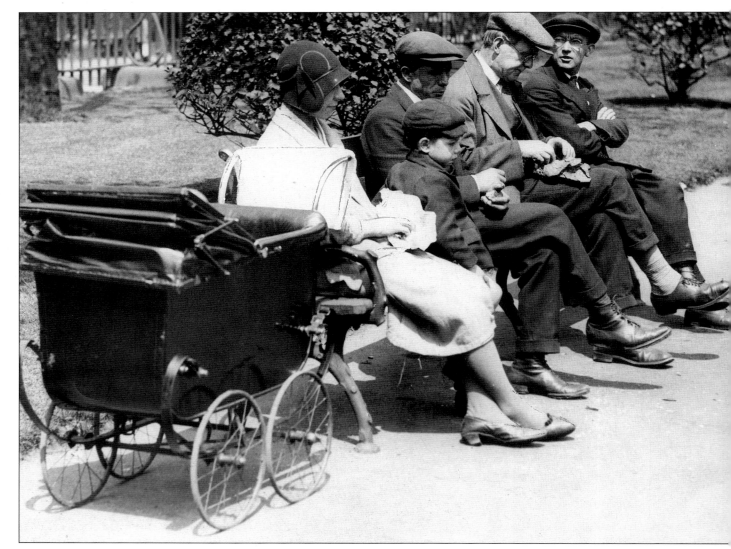

Lunchtime in St Philip's churchyard, 1932.

St. James Junior II School, Brewery Street, Handsworth, 1932.

Seymour Hicks is at the Birmingham Theatre Royal this week. There is also a farce-melodrama called "The Gay Adventure." But it is Seymour Hicks who matters: the play, here, is definitely not the thing.

Unquestionably, Seymour Hicks is an original. In his line there is no one like him: he defies the most sedulous and painstaking imitation. His style is unique, and in its astonishing combination of superb acting and impossible buffoonery it defies description.

BY MERE GESTURE

No man on the stage can suggest with a wink or the lifting of an eyebrow more of sheer salaciousness without any offence at all than Seymour Hicks; and few actors or comedians can achieve such drollery or be so excruciatingly comic by mere grimace or gesture alone.

Seymour Hicks is rather like a perky and very cheeky sparrow. His mind hops hither and thither with a delightful and insolent audacity, and his tongue follows in its wake with an unexpectedness of comment that is very fascinating.

He will be seen at the top of his form in "The Gay Adventure." This play is something of farce, something of melodrama, and also nearly a film. It might make an excellent example of either type of entertainment. As it is, however, it is just a hotch-potch vehicle for the genius of Seymour Hicks. And a very amusing mixed entertainment he makes it.

May Festival, Pitmaston Road School, Hall Green, 1932.

The Hall of Memory, 30th October 1932.

The world-famous concert pianist and former Premier of Poland, Ignace Jan Paderewski, arrives at New Street Station, 6th January 1933.

The Alpine Gardens, Botanical Gardens, Edgbaston, 1933.

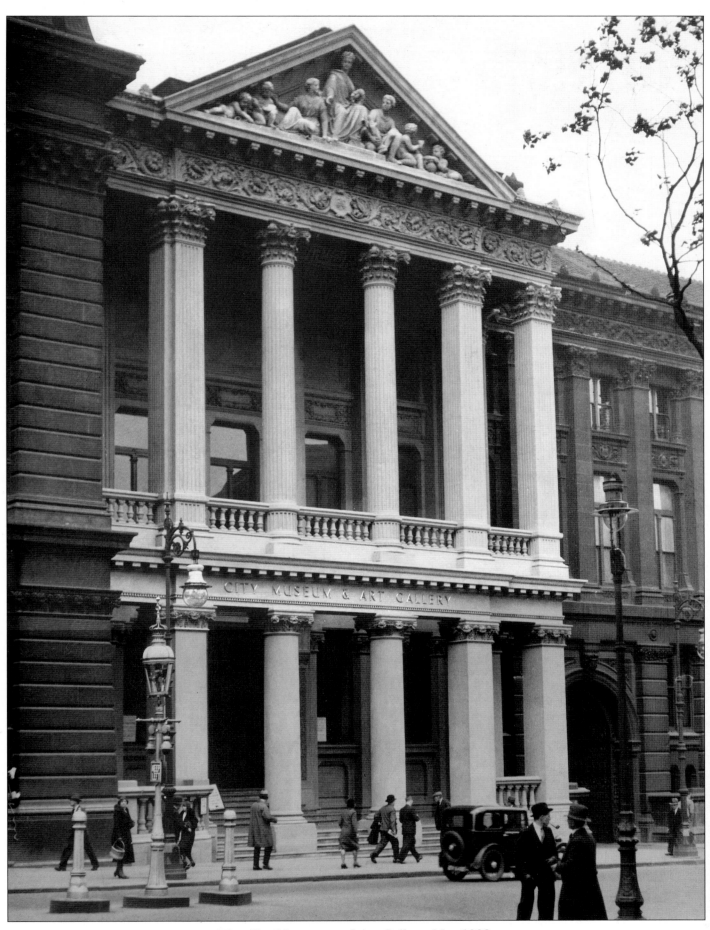

The City Museum and Art Gallery, May 1933.

Acocks Green Council School, Hartfield Crescent, 1933.

Park Garage (Moseley) Ltd., Alcester Road, Moseley, 1933.

The new premises of the Birmingham Municipal Bank, Church Road, Yardley, 13th May 1933.

Staff from the Weights and Measures Dept., testing petrol pumps, 1933.

Checking the weight of a vehicle's load on a Corporation weighbridge, 1933.

Great Western Arcade, 1933.

Bandleader, Duke Ellington, is greeted on arrival at the Hippodrome,
17th July 1933. Incidentally, the advert is for Foster Clark's Cream Custard.

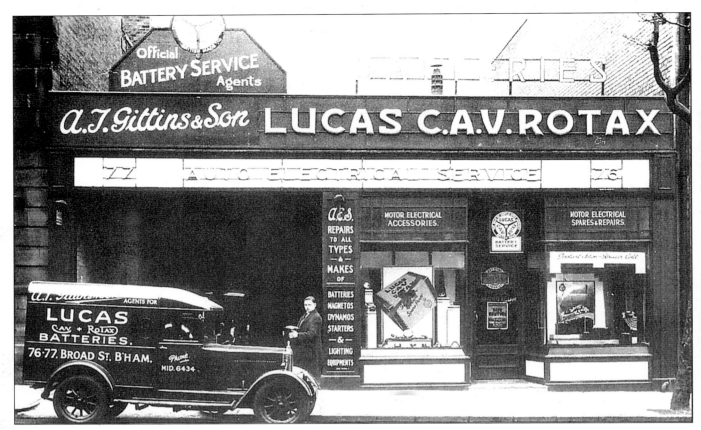

Broad Street, 1933.

The new paddling pool is put to good use, Lightwoods Park, 26th August 1933.

Road-widening in progress, Edgbaston Old Church, Church Road, 13th October 1933.

Parents' Day, Yardley Wood Infants' School, School Road, 1933. The play was "The Golden Fleece".

Sir Malcolm Campbell tries out the new safety cycle, Hercules Cycle and Motor Co. Ltd., Rocky Lane, Aston, 1933.

Just prior to the Grand Opening of the Olton cinema, Warwick Road, 29th September 1933.

The Ambulance Room, Joseph Lucas Ltd., Great King Street, Hockley, c. 1933.

Sir Oswald Mosley and his supporters in the city for a rally of Fascists, 14th November 1933.

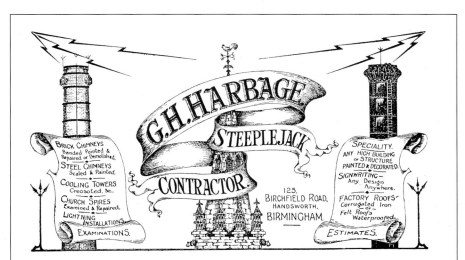

THE BIRMINGHAM MARKET HALL

Worcester Street Entrance

ENGLAND'S FINEST MARKET

The Market Hall Attractions

Nowhere can one hope to find the equal of that exceptional atmosphere of out-door comfort that surrounds those who have discovered the delights of shopping in the Birmingham Market Hall. Like Arcadia, that charming city of a beautiful myth, the City Market Hall, nestling in the very heart of the shopping centre of the Midlands, presents a wonderful galaxy of all that the most fastidious shopper can desire.

Shopping in this Market Hall is akin to shopping in an amazingly controlled large department store. There is scarcely any household requirement one cannot purchase there—every conceivable kind of merchandise in unthought of variety is not only there, but possessed of qualities, calculated to delight the eye, the ear, and the mind of every visitor. An assemblage of everything that the householder is likely to require drawn from every market of the world.

SPECIAL ! !

FLOWERS   FRUIT   FISH
AND
OTHER SHOWS
1934

Ratepayers! The MARKETS are yours, SHOP IN THEM

SHOP IN   THE CITY   MARKET HALL

HISTORY OF THE MARKET HALL.
By T. RENSHAW.

When Leland, somewhere between A.D. 1535 and 1543, "cam throughe a praty strete," the pretty street being "Drytey," i.e., Deritend, he was much impressed by the "bewty" of the "good market towne" of "Bremischam," which lay before him, and as he climbed the hill leading him on through the Bull Ring towards the High Street, he saw around him evidences of industry and busy-ness. "There be many smithes that use to make knives and all maner of cuttynge tooles," he observed, "many lorimars that make byts, and a greate many naylors," and concluded that "a greate parte of the towne is maytayned by smithes." If Leland's visit had chanced to be on a Thursday, he would have found the whole town occupied with the business of market day; he would have noted the rude stalls and booths in the Bull Ring, and the careless piles of goods and merchandise scattered at intervals along his route past the "paroche Church," which was the only Church he saw in the town. If his visit had been made 200 years later he would have noted that the town was still without a centralised market place, for in the Bull Ring he would have seen corn sampled, and garden produce for sale; farther up Spiceal Street he would have found butchers' stalls, while at the corner of Moor Street he might have purchased flowers or shrubs. Piles of earthenware would have obstructed his passage along the footpaths leading up to New Street, where horses, pigs and sheep would be standing; passing along High Street he would have noted the fruit, poultry, and butter on sale at the bottom of Bull Street, and in Dale End he would have found the Cattle Market. Still another century was to elapse before the scattered market was so organised as to confine it to something like a central position within a defined area.

But it must not be assumed from all this that Birmingham, though apparently backward in the 18th century, as in the 16th, was in reality non-progressive in the matter of market facilities, for when, in the 13th century there was something like a "boom" in market Charters, and over 3,000 places clamoured for market privileges, the Birmingham market was already well-established with a century or so of experience to its credit. It was the enterprising Peter de Birmingham, grandson of Richard—who held the manor in 1066, and probably for sixteen

years before then—who, in the year 1166, received from his over-lord, Gervase Paganel, Lord of Dudley, in the presence of King Henry II., the grant of a charter "to have market on Thursday at his castle of Burmingeham." The grant was made, it is believed, at Feckenham, where the restless King was hunting in the Royal Forest. It must not be supposed that the Castle of "Burmingeham" (there are a hundred and more ways of spelling this name of the town) was a lordly pile like Dudley Castle or others of that type in the Midlands; it was not more than a smallish, though perhaps rambling wooden structure on a low mound, surrounded by a stockade of timber and a moat. But the association of a market with that manor house or castle is perpetuated to-day, some 760 years later, by the fact that the present wholesale Fruit and Vegetable Market is erected on the same site, and when its boundary walls on Moat Lane and Moat Row were being constructed, they had to be carried down 14 feet to get below the accumulated mud and ooze of the ancient castle moat. All the Birmingham central markets of to-day lie in the immediate neighbourhood of "the Castle of Burmingeham." Other Charters followed the first one. King Richard Lion-heart, who is thought to have visited the town in November, 1189, made a further grant in that year; and in 1218, Roger Somery, Lord of Dudley, granted to the Burgesses of Dudley freedom of toll in Dudley, Wolverhampton, and Birmingham

markets. The first right to hold a fair in the town was granted in 1250 to William de Burmingham, by King Henry III., and it was this progressive de Birmingham who, as a member of the party of reform, joined Simon de Montfort, and, with his chief, was killed at the Battle of Evesham fifteen years later. The city's present motto, "Forward," is of modern adoption, but, as we have seen, its spirit has endured through long centuries.

There are now six markets in Birmingham: the Market Hall, the Bull Ring Market, the Wholesale Fruit and Vegetable Market, the Smithfield Market for Cattle, Horses, etc., the Dead Meat Market, and the Wholesale Fish Market; and of these the most popular amongst retail buyers and the general public are the ancient open-air market in the Bull Ring, and the Market Hall.

In 1806, the Commissioners of the Birmingham Street Act, the then governing body of the town, became contractors for the tolls and so obtained control of the market administration, and ten years later purchased the old Manor property for the purpose of a cattle market there, which was opened the following year; and in 1824-5 they purchased the manorial rights and tolls for £12,500, a

bargain which was to prove an invaluable investment on behalf of the inhabitants of the town. Fifty or sixty years later the tolls were yielding somewhere about £16,000 per annum. The Commissioners began to think of a Market Hall after they had acquired the tolls, and six public-spirited men, who were members of this organised governing body bought, at their own risk, 9,600 square yards of land at a cost of £44,800, for the purpose. When the necessary Act was obtained they transferred the land to the Commissioners at cost price, and on February 23, 1833, the first stone of the Market Hall was laid. The building cost £28,430, which sum, together with the cost of the land, brought the total expenditure up to £73,266. The building extends from the Bull Ring to Worcester Street, its length is 365 feet, its width 108 feet, and its height 60 feet. The Hall is laid out in four main avenues with narrower side avenues, and has accommodation for 600 stalls. In the "Gazette" of February 16, 1835, we read:

"The new Market Hall was thrown open to the public on Thursday last (February 12), and during the days it was crowded with persons, a considerable portion of whom were no doubt attracted by curiosity. On Saturday it was again visited by great numbers, and in the evening was lighted up with gas for the accommodation of buyers and sellers."

We may note that gas had been employed for the first time in Birmingham 33 years before by Murdoch at his factory, to celebrate by formal illuminations the Peace of Amiens.

Birmingham received its Municipal Charter in 1838, but it was not until 1851 that the Commissioners transferred to the Corporation their rights and powers in respect of the markets, and at that date they had spent nearly £106,000 on their market enterprises. We read that in this year a bronze fountain was erected in the centre of the Market Hall, and inaugurated on Christmas Eve, but of this fountain there is now no trace, and whether it was removed and re-erected elsewhere, or whether it was dismantled and sold does not appear to be recorded. It is to the Commissioners that we owe the possession of the several acres of land now known as Smithfield, and the vast organisation now under the control of the Markets Committee of the City Council has been built on the foundations laid so firmly by that energetic body of men to whom we of modern Birmingham owe so much.

36

Starbank Road School, Small Heath, c. 1934.

Burbury Street Infants' School, Lozells, c. 1934.

The Kitts family, from Yardley Wood, enjoy a break in
Weston-super-Mare, 1934.

JOSEPH CHAMBERLAIN MEMORIAL MUSEUM

HIGHBURY, MOOR GREEN
BIRMINGHAM

OPENING CEREMONY
MONDAY, 9TH JULY, 1934

JOSEPH CHAMBERLAIN MEMORIAL MUSEUM

OPENING BY
THE RT. HON. SIR AUSTEN CHAMBERLAIN, K.G., M.P.

ORDER OF PROCEEDINGS

The guests will assemble in the hall at 3 p.m.

The Lord Mayor (Alderman H. E. Goodby, J.P.) will take the Chair, and will ask the Rt. Hon. Sir Austen Chamberlain, K.G., M.P., to declare the Memorial Museum open.

The Rt. Hon. Sir Austen Chamberlain will speak.

Mr. Alderman W. A. Cadbury, Chairman of the Museum and Art Gallery Committee, will propose a vote of thanks to the Rt. Hon. Sir Austen Chamberlain, the Lord Mayor and the donors.

The Lord Mayor will accompany the members of the Chamberlain family to the Library, where the Rt. Hon. Neville Chamberlain, M.P., will unveil a memorial tablet erected by the Highbury Trustees. The tablet bears the following inscription :

"The Rt. Hon. Joseph Chamberlain, M.P., resided in this House from 1880 until his death in London in 1914. From 1915 until 1918 the House was used as a Military Hospital by permission of Sir Austen Chamberlain, K.G., M.P., who in 1919 generously gave the whole of the buildings to the Highbury Trustees, who by means of voluntary contributions purchased the land forming the Highbury Estate. From 1919 to 1932 the premises were used as a Hospital for Disabled Ex-Service Men, when the Estate was given by the Trustees to the Birmingham City Council for the general benefit of the citizens. The Library in which Joseph Chamberlain constantly worked and read, and where he prepared some of his most famous speeches and entertained many distinguished guests, has been preserved in his memory. July, 1934."

The Library will be open for inspection by the guests from 4 to 6 o'clock.

Between the same hours tea will be served in the Day Room and Fernery, by invitation of the Highbury Trustees.

The Home for aged women will be open to inspection till 6 p.m. by invitation of the Public Assistance Committee.

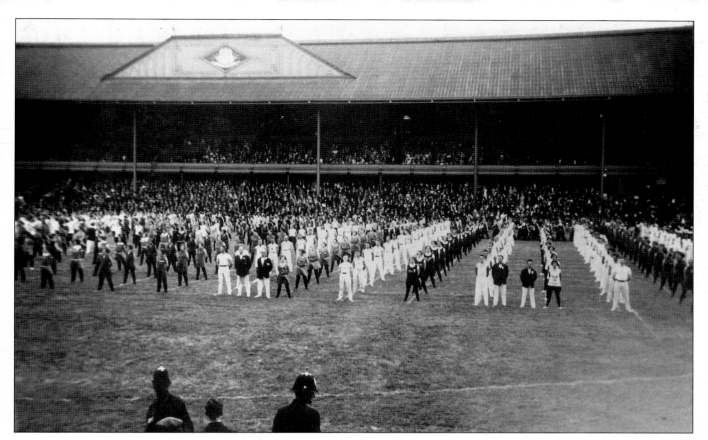

The Birmingham and District Amateur Gymnastics Association takes part in the Birmingham Sports Carnival, Villa Park, 14th July 1934.

Gymnasts taking part in the 52nd Birmingham Charity Sports Carnival, Villa Park, 14th July 1934.

The Rose Hill Ladies Golf team, winners of the Birmingham Gazette Cup, 1934.

Girls involved in inspection work, The Triplex Safety Glass Co. Ltd., Kings Norton, c. 1934.

A plaque is erected to commemorate the centenary of the opening of the Town Hall. 27th September 1934.

The view through the Town Hall portico, from Ratcliff Place to Galloways Corner, 3rd October 1934.

A rare sight today. These beautiful ornamental gates had just been erected to the memory of Coun. Frederick Tippetts, at Moseley Parish Church and dedicated by the Bishop of Birmingham, 11th October 1934.

Birmingham Air Port Approved

THE Ministry of Transport has approved the application of the City Council for compulsory powers to purchase a site on the Coventry Road, at Elmdon, for a Civic Airport.

Work is to be commenced on the ground immediately.

It is understood that hangars are to be built which will make provision for private aeroplanes, and it is expected that the Midland Aero Club will transfer its headquarters from Castle Bromwich to Elmdon.

Opening day arrives for the Birmingham Settlement (Kingstanding Branch) Kingstanding Road, 29th October 1934.

42   A reception for the new secretary of the YMCA, W.G. Cadenhead (extreme left), Dale End, 14th December 1934.

Prince of Wales Theatre, Broad Street, 1934. This area is now part of the ICC site.

The Alexandra Theatre, John Bright Street, 1934.

1935

Employees of the Public Works Dept., at the annual dinner of the Deritend Occupational Centre, held at Floodgate Street School, 4th January 1935.

Worcester Street entrance to the Market Hall, 6th February 1935.

The Old Smithy, Church Road, with Church Terrace on the immediate left, Yardley, 1935.

The recently-created roundabout island at the junction of Stratford Road/Sandy Lane/Camp Hill, 13th February 1935.

The Silver Jubilee official royal portrait, May 1935. From left to right: The Prince of Wales, the Princess Royal, the Duke of Gloucester, King George V, the Duke of York, Queen Mary, the Duke of Kent.

Silver Jubilee Party, Fosbrooke Road, Small Heath, 1935.

As part of the Silver Jubilee celebrations residen from Miller Street and Bracebridge Street, Astor enjoy a trip to the Lickey Hills, May 1935.

Silver Jubilee party, North Road, Selly Oak, with the Boxfoldia factory at the end of the road, May 1935.

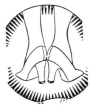

The illuminated tramcar, commemorating the Silver Jubilee of King George V, sets out on its first trip, 7th May 1935.

The great comedian, George Robey, serenades Alice Delysia, in the production, "Accidentally Yours", Theatre Royal, 3rd June 1935.

Deritend Bridge, another landmark about to disappear, 8th June 1935.

All ready for the opening of the Odeon, Kingstanding, 22nd July 1935.

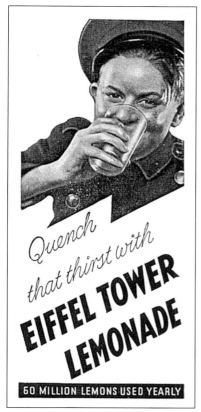

Bearwood Road Junior School, 1935.

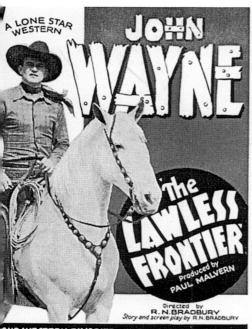
Acocks Green Junior School, Warwick Road, 1935.

Hamstead Hall, Hamstead Hall Avenue, is up for sale
(for demolition), Great Barr, 1935.

Renovations at the Town Hall, 28th August 1935.

Removing the gigantic figures in the Imperial Arcade, Dale End, 9th October 1935.
They were moved to the Market Hall, in the Bull Ring, where they became part of the clock.

1936

The horse trough at the junction of Icknield Street/New Spring Street, Hockley, c. 1936.

Film star, Anna Neagle, visits the Gaumont cinema, Steelhouse Lane, 12th January 1936.

City Arcade, looking towards Kunzle's Cafe Royal, in Union Street, 11th February 1936.

The framework of the new municipal baths, Bristol Road South,
Northfield, February 1936.

Engineers overhaul "Big Brum", the landmark clock that dominates
Chamberlain Square, 2nd March 1936.

The Lord Mayor, Ald. Samuel Grey, inspects the restoration work taking
place in the ruins of Weoley Castle, 24th April 1936.

THE ROLL CALL
Complete Table of Players called upon, and chief Goal Scorers for Season 1935-36.
FIRST DIVISION.

Club	Players called on	Ever-present	Chief Scorer	No. of Goals
Arsenal	29	0	Drake	23
Aston Villa	30	0	Astley	19
Birmingham	27	1	Jones	20
Blackburn Rovers	31	1	Thompson	15
Bolton Wanderers	23	1	Milsom	20
Brentford	24	2	McCulloch	26
Chelsea	26	0	Bambrick	15
Derby County	24	2	Gallacher	15
Everton	23	0	Cunliffe	23
Grimsby Town	21	3	Glover	31
Huddersfield Town	24	1	Lythgoe	15
Leeds United	25	0	Kelly (J)	15
Liverpool	28	0	Howe	18
Manchester City	22	1	Brook	13
Middlesbrough	23	2	Camsell	28
Portsmouth	25	0	Weddle	16
Preston North End	17	4	Maxwell	17
Sheffield Wednesday	25	1	Dewar	19
Stoke City	19	3	Sale	14
Sunderland	23	2	Carter & Gurney each	31
West Bromwich Albion	27	0	Richardson (W G)	39
Wolverhampton W	29	2	Wrigglesworth	12

Warwickshire C.C.C., May 1936.

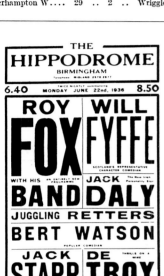

Cadbury's new swimming baths, 1936.

The proposed site for the new Civic Centre building, between the Hall of Memory and Cambridge Street, 1936.

St. Chad's Roman Catholic Cathedral, Bath Street, 1936.

Ernest Boyce outside the family business, Cox Street West,
Balsall Heath, c. 1936.

Cleaning the Joseph Chamberlain Memorial,
Chamberlain Square, 1936.

The Prince of Wales meets members of the Distinguished Conduct Medal League, Victoria Square, 23rd July 1936.

Islington Row, 1936.

Alterations to the traffic island, Victoria Square/New Street, 14th August 1936.

The Rock, Alum Rock Road, 1936.

Gentlemanly Sport

THE absence of professionalism in a game tends to add to the interest of the contest.

This feeling was especially marked at Kent-street Baths during the international judo (perhaps you will more easily recognise it as jiu-jitsu) match between Germany and Birmingham.

From various talks I had with individual spectators, I gathered that the majority of them were seeing the sport for the first time.

Certainly they were not well up in all its higher points, but they could appreciate talent and skill and sportsmanship—and there is no more gentlemanly sport under the sun than judo—to the full, and voiced their feelings without prejudice to either side.

There was none of that partisan, unfair spirit that decrie the winner because he doesn't happen to be your own man.

The Germans received a rousing welcome, and a hearty cheer, for their victory.

Production at the Austin works is speeded up to fulfill demand, Longbridge, 24th August 1936.

The Lord Mayor, Ald. Samuel Grey, opens the new Municipal Bank, Longbridge, 8th September 1936.

"Fernbank", Alum Rock Road, about to become the siting for two of the city's anti-aircraft batteries, December 1936.

Gilbertstone Hall, Coventry Road, Yardley, 1936.

"A Christmas Carol", Boulton Road Junior School, Handsworth, 1936.

"Julius Caesar", King Edward's Grammar School, Frederick Road,
Aston, 10th December 1936.

Class 9, St Mark's Central Public Elementary School, King Edward's Road, Ladywood, 1936.

THE KING ABDICATES

Mrs. Simpson.

Mr. Baldwin's Statement in the Commons

KING EDWARD HAS MADE HIS DECISION. HE IS TO GIVE UP THE THRONE.

MR. BALDWIN ANNOUNCED THIS DECISION TO A CROWDED HOUSE OF COMMONS THIS AFTERNOON

Edward VIII.

SENSATIONAL SPEECH BY MR. BALDWIN

"The King Told Me, 'I Am Going To Marry Mrs. Simpson And I Am Prepared To Go'"

NEWS

is big this week. For the next few days the " Evening Despatch " will be in exceptional demand. To avoid disappointment **PLACE YOUR ORDER NOW**

SOUVENIR OF 1936 — THE YEAR OF THE THREE KINGS

H.M. KING GEORGE V. Accession May 6 1910 Died Jan 20 1936

H.M. KING GEORGE VI. Accession Dec 11 1936 Coronation Day May 12 1937

H.M. KING EDWARD VIII Accession Jan 20 1936 Abdication Dec 11 1936

Olton Boulevard East/Warwick Road, Acocks Green, December 1936.

60

Stoney Lane, Sparkbrook, 6th January 1937. After thirty years this was the last day for the Stratford Road route.

Albert Street/Moor Street, 19th January 1937. The building was about to be converted into a Salvation Army Hostel.

Coronation party, Somerville Road, Small Heath, 1937.

A FORM OF PRAYER
AND
THANKSGIVING
TO
ALMIGHTY GOD

commended by the

ARCHBISHOPS OF
CANTERBURY AND YORK

for general use on
WEDNESDAY, THE 12th DAY OF MAY, 1937
being the day of the Coronation of their Majesties

KING GEORGE VI
AND
QUEEN ELIZABETH
IN THE
ABBEY CHURCH OF ST. PETER, WESTMINSTER

LONDON 1937
Printed by EYRE AND SPOTTISWOODE LIMITED
Printers to the King's most Excellent Majesty

Celebrating the Coronation of King George VI the workforce
decorate their workshop at their own expense, Joseph Lucas Ltd.,
Great King Street, Hockley, 12th May 1937.

All ready for the Coronation party, Tinkers Farm School, Northfield, May 1937.

Corporation Street, with Union Street first on the right, May 1937.

New Street, 1937.

Moseley Parish Church all lit up for the Coronation, 1937.

Gymnastics at Summer Lane Girls School, 1937.

Cherrywood Road Junior School football team, winners of the
Birmingham Schools Shield, 1937.

The Maypole cinema gets ready for its opening, later in the day,
Alcester Road South, Kings Heath, 1st July 1937.

Harborne Collegiate School for Boys, Court Oak Road, c. 1937.

Highgate tram depot, 1937.

Bristol Road South, with Bournville Lane on the right, Summer 1937.

ADELPHI, Hay Mills (A.B.C.). VIC. 1208.
VICTOR McLAGLEN, PETER LORRE in "NANCY STEELE IS MISSING" (A).
Also
PATRICK WADDINGTON in "BLACK TULIP" (A).
Free Car Park.

ALBION, NEW INNS, HANDSWORTH.
Large Car Park.
JESSIE MATTHEWS in the Most Entertaining Film of her career. "EVERGREEN" (A), with SONNIE HALE and BETTY BALFOUR. Also: ALEXANDER CARR and DICKEY MOORE in "DIVINE LOVE."

ALHAMBRA, Camp Hill (A.B.C.). VIC. 2826.
JAMES MELTON,
HUGH HERBERT, ZASU PITTS in
"COME UP SMILING" (U).
PHIL REGAN in "HAPPY GO LUCKY" (U).

APOLLO, TYBURN ROAD, PYPE HAYES.
All Seats Bookable. 'Phone: ERD. 0834.
SYDNEY HOWARD, "SPLINTERS IN THE AIR" (U). "SPLINTERS" . . . in the R.A.F.! Also: Jane Wyatt in "LUCKIEST GIRL IN THE WORLD" (U). Thursday: "Please, Teacher" (U). Car Parks. Harold Moore at the Organ.

ASTORIA, Aston (A.B.C.). ASTon 2384.
JACK BENNY, BURNS and ALLEN,
"COLLEGE HOLIDAY" (U).
WILSON BARRETT,
"CONCERNING MR. MARTIN" (A).

BIRCHFIELD PICTURE HOUSE.
Mats. each day at 2.45. Jean Harlow, Robert Taylor in "Man in Possession" (U). Jean Harlow and Robert Taylor co-starred for the first and only time. "Life Hesitates at 40." "The March of Time, No. 12." Two perf. Sat. eve. at 6 and 8.30. You may Reserve Seats in Balcony.

BROADWAY CINEMA, Bristol St. MID. 1761.
PAUL CAVANAGH and GRETA NISSEN in
"CAFE COLETTE" (A).
Also: MAE CLARKE and JOHN PAYNE in
"HATS OFF" (U).
Thurs. Next: "MORE THAN A SECRETARY" (A).

CAPITOL CINEMA, ALUM ROCK.
NOAH BEERY and BESSIE LOVE in
"LIVE AGAIN" (A).
PAUL ROBESON in "MY SONG GOES FORTH" (U).
Thursday: GENE GERRARD in "SUCH IS LIFE" (A); RONALD FRANKAU in "INTERNATIONAL REVUE" (U).

CARLTON, TAUNTON ROAD, SPARKBROOK.
Mats. Mon., Wed., Thurs., Sat. 13A 'Bus.
JANE WITHERS with SLIM SUMMERVILLE in
"CAN THIS BE DIXIE?" (U).
BEN LYON in "DOWN TO THE SEA" (A).
Thurs.: "SPLINTERS IN THE AIR" (U) (Sydney Howard).

CORONET, SMALL HEATH. VICtoria 0420.
RICHARD TAUBER in "PAGLIACCI" (A).
RICHARD TAUBER in "PAGLIACCI" (A).
With STEFFI DUNA and DIANA NAPIER.
Thurs.: "Once A Doctor" (A); "It's Not Cricket" (A).

CROWN, Ladywood (A.B.C.). EDGbaston 1122.
PAT O'BRIEN in "THE GREAT O'MALLEY" (U), with HUMPHREY BOGART and SYBIL JASON. Also BILLY MAUCH in "PENROD AND SAM" (A). Thursday Next: "CALLING ALL STARS" (U), with LARRY ADLER, FLOTSAM and JETSAM.

DELICIA, GOSTA GREEN.
To-day: A wonderful programme again, folks! ZASU PITTS and HUGH HERBERT in "COME UP SMILING" (U); also "YELLOW CARGO" (U), with CONRAD NAGEL. Cunning Chinks and Cops. Thursday next: "PLUCK OF THE IRISH" (A), also "TICKET TO PARADISE" (A).

ELITE, SOHO ROAD, HANDSWORTH.
To-day: NOR. 0665
EDWARD G. ROBINSON in
"THUNDER IN THE CITY" (U).
And Full Programme.
Thurs.: "Melody For Two" (U) and "It's Not Cricket" (A).

EMPRESS, SUTTON COLDFIELD. SUT. 2363.
Enormous Free Car Park. To-day: Max Miller in "Don't Get Me Wrong" (U), with Olive Blackney and George Stone. The Craziest and Funniest Comedy of the Season. Screening at 3.58, 6.48 & 9.41. Also "The Richest Girl in the World" (U), with Jane Wyatt and Louis Hayward. Matinee Daily at 2.30.

ERA CINEMA, BORDESLEY GREEN.
Tel.: VIC. 0543. Free Car Park and Cycle Shed. Mats. Mon., Wed., Thurs., 2.30. Eves cont., doors open 6.0. FRANCES DAY in "DREAMS COME TRUE" (A); George O'Brien in "O'Malley of the Mounted" (U). Thurs.: Maurice Chevalier in "The Beloved Vagabond" (A).

GRAND, ALUM ROCK, SALTLEY. EASt 0471.
"CAREER WOMAN" (A).
with CLAIRE TREVOR, MICHAEL WHALEN.
Also "WHITE HUNTER" (A).
with WARNER BAXTER, JUNE LANG.

GRANGE, SMALL HEATH. VICtoria 0434.
SHIRLEY TEMPLE IN
"STOWAWAY" (U).
Supported by a Musical Revue—
"CARRY ON, LONDON," and News.

GROVE CINEMA, DUDLEY ROAD. SME. 0343
Mats. at 2.30. Evenings continuous from 6 o'clock. "THE GREAT O'MALLEY" (U), with PAT O'BRIEN. Also "PENROD AND SAM" (A), with BILLY MAUCH. Sunday next: "THIS IS THE LIFE" (U), with JANE WITHERS. Also "IN OLD KENTUCKY" (U).

IMPERIAL, Moseley Road (A.B.C.). CAL. 2283.
JOSEPH CALLEIA and FLORENCE RICE in
"MAN OF THE PEOPLE" (A).
Also ANN DVORAK and HARRY CAREY in
"RACING LADY" (U).

KINGSTON, SMALL HEATH. VIC. 2639.
Car Park. All the Week:—
A Terrific Musical-Variety Show,
"CALLING ALL STARS" (U).
With AMBROSE, LARRY ADLER, BILLY BENNETT, Etc.
Gene Autry in "THE SINGING COWBOY" (U).

KINGSWAY, KING'S HEATH.
SOUth 1352. Car Park. JAMES MELTON in "MELODY FOR TWO" (U). HUGH WILLIAMS in "SIDE STREET ANGEL" (A). Thurs.: "Devil's Playground" (A); "Counterfeit Lady" (U). Mats. Daily (except Fri.). Eves. cont. from 6 (inc. Sat.). Book'g Sat. discontinued.

LYRIC PICTURE PLAYHOUSE, PARADE.
Four minutes from the Town Hall.
TALA BIRRELL, "SHE'S DANGEROUS" (A),
CÆSAR ROMERO, "SHE'S DANGEROUS" (A).
Also NOAH BEERY in "THE MIGHTY TREVE" (U).
Thurs.: JANE WITHERS, "CAN THIS BE DIXIE" (U).

MAJESTIC, BEARWOOD.
"WAKE UP FAMOUS" (U),
With GENE GERRARD and NELSON KEYS.
Also "SHE'S DANGEROUS" (A).
With TALA BIRELL and CESAR ROMERO.
Thursday: "Criminal Lawyer" (A), also "Racing Lady" (U).

MAYFAIR, Kingstanding. ERDington 1773.
Matinees daily 2.30. Evenings continuous from 6.0.
Deaf Patrons catered for.
JEAN ARTHUR in "MORE THAN A SECRETARY" (A).
Also MARY BRIAN in "KILLER AT LARGE" (A).

MAYPOLE CINEMA, KING'S HEATH.
WARstock 2051. Free Car Park.
GEORGE FORMBY in
"OFF THE DOLE" (A).
Mats. Daily except Tues. and Fri. Eves. Cont. from 6.
Admission 6d. 9d. 1s. 1s. 3d. (including tax).

NORTHFIELD CINEMA. 'Phone: PRIory 1463
RICHARD ARLEN and LILI PALMER in
"THE GREAT BARRIER" (U).
Also BUSTER KEATON in "GRAND SLAM OPERA" (U).
Thursday: "PLUCK OF THE IRISH" (A).

OAK, Selly Oak (A.B.C.). SELly Oak 0139.
LIONEL BARRYMORE in
"A FAMILY AFFAIR" (A).
CLAUDE HULBERT in "THE VULTURE" (A).
Thursday: JACK BENNY in "COLLEGE HOLIDAY" (U).

ODEON, BIRCHFIELD ROAD, PERRY BARR.
BIR. 4453. AMBROSE & HIS BAND in "CALLING ALL STARS" (U), at 3.55, 6.35, 9.15. Donald Cook and Judith Allen in "BEWARE OF LADIES" (A), at 2.40, 5.20 and 8.0. Silly Symphony Cartoon, "MOTHER PLUTO" (U)

ODEON, KINGSTANDING. SUTton 2551.
SANDY POWELL and GINA MALO in
"IT'S A GRAND OLD WORLD" (U) at 3.42, 7.12, 9.40. HUGH WILLIAMS & LEONORA CORBETT in "HAPPY FAMILY" (A), at 2.30, 6.0, 8.28. Mats. daily 2.30. Eves. cont. from 6. Sat. 6 & 8.30. 9d., 1/-, 1/3, balcony bookable.

ODEON, SHIRLEY. Tel.: SHIrley 1183.
"GOLD DIGGERS OF 1937" (U). The Show of Shows, with Dick Powell, Joan Blondell, Glenda Farrell, and All-Star Cast. Showing 2.10, 4.25, 6.30, 8.50. Donald Cook in "Beware of Ladies" (A), Gaumont British News. Cont. from 2 Daily. Sat. Mat. 2.15. Sat. Evening, 5.40, 8.25.

ODEON, SUTTON COLDFIELD. SUTton 2714.
Continuous Daily from 2.30. Car Park.
"GOLD DIGGERS OF 1937" (U).
At 3.25, 6.15, 9.5.
Also "THE LADY REPORTER" (A), at 2.30, 5.20, 8.10.
News 5.5 and 8.0. Next week: "STOWAWAY" (U).

OLTON CINEMA, WARWICK RD. ACO. 0593.
To-day: NELSON KEYS & GENE GERRARD, "WAKE UP FAMOUS" (A), and MARGOT GRAHAME in "NIGHT WAITRESS" (A). Thurs next: Jean Arthur & George Brent, "More Than a Secretary" (A). Mat. Mon., Wed., Thurs. at 2.30 (Children mat. Sat.). Mon. to Fri. even. cont. from 6.15.

ORIENT, Aston (A.B.C.). NORthern 1615.
SONJA HENIE in "ONE IN A MILLION" (U), with ADOLPHE MENJOU, JEAN HERSHOLT, DON AMECHE, NED SPARKS, RITZ BROS., ARLENE GUDGE. Sunday: "THE GHOST GOES WEST" (A), SHAKE-DOWN" (A).

PALACE, Bordesley (A.B.C.). VICtoria 1830.
JOSEPH CALLEIA FLORENCE RICE TED HEALY
"MAN OF THE PEOPLE" (A).
ANN DVORAK in "RACING LADY" (U).

PALACE, Erdington (A.B.C.). ERDington 1623
CLAUDETTE COLBERT with FRED MACMURRAY
in "MAID OF SALEM" (A).
Also VICTOR JORY in ZANE GREY'S
"RANGLE RIVER" (U).
Thurs.: "John Meade's Woman" (A), "Everything in Life" (U)

PALLADIUM, Hockley (A.B.C.). NOR 0380.
LIONEL BARRYMORE and CECILIA PARKER in
"A FAMILY AFFAIR" (A).
In addition: NOAH BEERY Jnr. in
"THE MIGHTY TREVE" (U).
Continuous Daily from 2.30.

PICTURE HOUSE, KNOWLE. 'Phone 2427.
JEAN HARLOW in
"SUZY" (A).
Thursday Next: "PENNIES FROM HEAVEN" (U).

PLAZA, Stockland Green. ERDington 1048.
Mats. Mon., Wed., Thurs. & Sat. 2.30. Eves. 5.45. Sat. 5.45 and 8.30. Balcony bookable. SYDNEY HOWARD in "SPLINTERS IN THE AIR" (U). JANE WYATT in "LUCKIEST GIRL IN THE WORLD" (U). Thursday: "Wake Up Famous" (U). and "Night Waitress" (A).

REGAL, Handsworth (A.B.C.). NOR. 1801.
SONJA HENIE, ADOLPHE MENJOU,
RITZ BROTHERS in
"ONE IN A MILLION" (U).
Eric Lord at Birmingham's Largest Cinema Organ.

RIALTO, HALL GREEN. SPRingfield 1270.
ROLAND YOUNG and CHILI BOUCHIER in
"GYPSY" (A).
Also a personal appearance of Miss Aloha Baker, the famous Hollywood traveller, who will describe her thrilling experiences while her film is being shown.

RITZ, Bordesley Green East (A.B.C.).
VICTOR McLAGLEN and PETER LORRE in
"NANCY STEELE IS MISSING" (A).
Also PATRICK WADDINGTON in "BLACK TULIP" (A).
Free Car Park. VIC. 1070.

ROBIN HOOD, Hall Green (A.B.C.). SPR. 2371
VICTOR McLAGLEN and PETER LORRE in
"NANCY STEELE IS MISSING" (A).
Also
GORDON HARKER in "BEAUTY AND THE BARGE" (U).

ROCK, ALUM ROCK ROAD, SALTLEY.
Free Car Park. Matinees daily except Friday.
ANN HARDING and BASIL RATHBONE in
"LOVE FROM A STRANGER" (A)
and full supporting programme.
Thurs.: "Splinters in the Air" (U). "Mysterious Crossing" (A).

ROYALTY, Harborne (A.B.C.). HAR. 1619.
SONJA HENIE,
ADOLPHE MENJOU — RITZ BROS.
IN
"ONE IN A MILLION" (U).

SAVOY, PERSHORE ROAD. Tel.: KIN. 1069.
Matinees Wednesday Only, 2.30. Car Park.
RICHARD ARLEN and LILLI PALMER in
"THE GREAT BARRIER" (U).
Also WILLIAM GARGAN in "NAVY BORN" (U).
Thurs.: Bobby Breen in "RAINBOW ON THE RIVER" (U).

SOLIHULL PICTURE HOUSE. SOLihull 0398
High Street, Solihull. Free Car Park.
WILL HAY in
"WINDBAG THE SAILOR" (U).
Also RALPH MORGAN in "YELLOWSTONE" (A).
Thurs.: "GREAT BARRIER" (U), RICHARD ARLEN.

SPRINGFIELD, STRATFORD RD. SPR. 1211.
WHEELER and WOOLSEY in
"MUMMY'S BOYS" (A).
Also RAY WALKER in "LADY REPORTER" (A).
Thurs.: Robert Armstrong in "WITHOUT ORDERS" (U).

STAR CINEMA, SLADE ROAD,
Gravelly Hill. Tel.: EASt 0461.
Mats. Mon., Wed., Thurs., Sat.
"AREN'T MEN BEASTS" (A), ROBERTSON HARE.
"AREN'T MEN BEASTS" (A), JUNE CLYDE.
Also "HARD ROCK HARRIGAN" (U).

TIVOLI PLAYHOUSE, COVENTRY ROAD.
AMBROSE and HIS ORCHESTRA, LARRY ADLER, BILLY BENNETT, FLOTSAM and JETSAM, etc., etc., in
"CALLING ALL STARS" (U).
GENE AUTRY in "THE SINGING COWBOY" (U).
Sun.: "SMART MONEY" (A), "NIGHT NURSE" (A).

TOWER, West Bromwich (A.B.C.). WES. 1210.
— SONJA HENIE —
"ONE IN A MILLION" (U).
With Adolphe Menjou, Jean Hersholt, Ned Sparks.
— Leslie Taff at the Tower Organ —
Continuous Daily from 2 o'clock. Free Car Park.

TUDOR, King's Heath (A.B.C.). HIG. 2861.
VICTOR McLAGLEN and PETER LORRE
IN
"NANCY STEELE IS MISSING" (A).
Also: SPRING BYINGTON in "PENROD AND SAM" (A).
Thursday: "COLLEGE HOLIDAY" (U), Jack Benny.

VICTORIA PLAYHOUSE, ASTON.
Cars 3x and 5 pass the door. JAMES MELTON and MARIE WILSON in "MELODY FOR TWO" (U). TALA BIRELL and CESAR ROMERO in "SHE'S DANGEROUS" (A). Thurs.: "MAGNIFICENT BRUTE" (U), "WHITE LEGION" (A).

WALDORF CINEMA, Sparkbrook. VIC. 0503.
"UNDER COVER OF NIGHT" (A) with
EDMUND LOWE, FLORENCE RICE.
"REASONABLE DOUBT" (A) with
JOHN STUART, MARJORIE TAYLOR.

WARLEY ODEON, HAGLEY ROAD WEST.
Tel. BEAwood 1549.
Dick Powell & Joan Blondell in "Gold Diggers of 1937" (U). daily at 3.17, 6.17, 9.17. Also: Donald Cooke with Judith Allen in "Beware of Ladies" (U), at 2.0, 5.0, 8.0
Cont. from 2 p.m. daily. Sat. mat. 2.15. Sat eve. 5.40 & 8.25

WARWICK CINEMA. ACOck's Green 0766.
Rochelle Hudson and Edward Norris and Caesar Romero in "TAINTED MONEY" (A).
Also: "UNDER YOUR SPELL" (U).
Thursday next: "White Hunter" (A).

WEOLEY CINEMA, WEOLEY CASTLE.
Car Park. Universal News. Matinees Mon. & Thurs. James Cagney, Mae Clark in "PLUCK OF THE IRISH" (A) also: George O'Brien in "O'Malley Of The Mounted" (U). Thursday: Tom Walls, Diana Churchill in "Dishonour Bright" (A).

WINDSOR THEATRE, BEARWOOD.
ROCHELLE HUDSON and CESAR ROMERO in
"TAINTED MONEY" (A).
Also LAWRENCE TIBBETT and WENDY BARRIE in
"UNDER YOUR SPELL" (U).
Thurs.: "Mama Steps Out" (A); "Mysterious Crossing" (A).

WINSON GREEN PICTURE PALACE,
Winson Green Road. 'Phone: NORthern 1790.
The funniest farce you've ever seen.
"AREN'T MEN BEASTS" (A).
With ROBERTSON HARE and ALFRED DRAYTON.

Central Fire Station competition team, shield and cup winners, 1937.

Early warning signs of possible conflict start to appear,
Town Hall, 1937.

Comedian, Sandy Powell (with pipe) is welcomed to the Forum
cinema for the showing of his film, "Leave It To Me",
New Street, 30th September 1937.

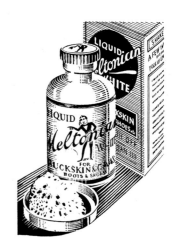

Work progresses on St Bartholomew's Parish Church, Hoggs Lane, Northfield, 6th October 1937.

Born in Middleton Hall Road, Kings Norton, actor
Brian Aherne, stars with Olivia De Havilland in
the film, "The Great Garrick", 1937.

Lord Nuffield (extreme right) holds the keys to the new
car presented to him by workers at Wolseley Motors Ltd.,
Drews Lane, Ward End, 20th December 1937.

Imperial Hotel, Temple Street, 1937.

Cock Sparrow Hall, St Margaret's Road, Ward End,
just prior to demolition, December 1937.

Bull Ring, 1937.

A nativity play, Fentham Road Girls School, Erdington, December 1937.

Unprecedented arrangements for dealing with the flood of Christmas letters and parcels in Birmingham have been brought into operation by the Postmaster-Surveyor (Mr. T. B. Braund). Not only have the staffs been augmented as never before, in order to avoid congestion of mail and parcel traffic through lack of man-power, but an entirely new sorting and distributing organisation has been superimposed upon the existing postal system.

The temporary staff taken on this Christmas numbers no fewer than 4,600. The staff of sorting clerks has been augmented by 2,000 temporary men (compared with 1,000 last year) and the temporary postmen number 2,600 (compared with 1,800 last year), so that the seasonal increase is 1,800 more than last Christmas.

Because accommodation at the General Post Office is inadequate for the flood of traffic expected, and in order to dispose of inward and outward mails as expeditiously as possible, a large system of decentralisation has been introduced. This has necessitated a big increase in the number of district sorting offices. There are now, for ordinary normal Post Office working, fourteen district sorting offices in the outer areas, and to meet Christmas pressure these have been supplemented by nineteen temporary letter and parcel sorting and delivery offices, fitted up in halls and schools.

Highfield Road, Hall Green, 1937.

ENTERTAINMENT FOR BLIND CHILDREN

Christmas brings joy to children, but possibly in an added measure to those afflicted with blindness. At the Birmingham Royal Institution for the Blind, which is responsible for the care and education of children of various ages, the pupils yesterday gave their Christmas entertainment in a manner that reflected the true spirit of the season. The gymnasium, where the entertainment took place, was gaily decorated with flags, streamers and holly; and the children, whose ages ranged from eleven to sixteen years, provided an entertainment which not only possessed artistic merit but radiated the happiness of lives undimmed by an abiding affliction. There were pianoforte solos, songs, dances, carols, choral singing and the performance by eight pupils of a play, "The Playgoers."

Fire damage at L.H. Newton & Co. Ltd., Thimble Mill Lane, Nechells, 23rd December 1937.

CHRISTMAS CIRCUS AT BINGLEY HALL

AMUSEMENT FOR ADULT AND CHILD AUDIENCES

Four centuries of the circus constitute a continuous period of development so leisurely that one hesitates to acclaim a new show as marking the birth of a new tendency. And yet, in recording the return of Miss A. M. Chapman's Christmas Circus to Bingley Hall for a month's run, beginning yesterday, one is bound to recognise the strain of sophistication that has crept into a form of entertainment most beloved by the ingenuous. Perhaps it is because the sawdust itself has gone, and in its place lies a fawn floor covering; perhaps the brilliant electric lights suspended from the roof of the hall are more reminiscent of the stage than of the "big top"; but assuredly it is due in part to the invasion of vaudeville acts into the circus ring. Lions may be as intelligent as men; horses may dance as nimbly as young girls; performing elephants may display the ponderous tractability of flattered dowagers; but unless the circus contains dancing girls and performers on the violin, the saxophone, the xylophone or what not, the tired business man may be caught yawning. These acts are as indispensable to adults as clowns are to youngsters; and the policy of the successful circus is to keep as many of the mixed adult and child audience laughing as much of the time as possible.

There are always acrobats to thrill old and young alike, and that is why Les Six Cristiani are likely to remain longest in the memories of those who see this 1937 Christmas Circus. Their springboard acrobatics are magnificent; their style superb. Like a breath from the old-time circus, too, come the Baker Boys, with their bare-back riding; and the daring leaps of Les Zerbinis through the hoop of fire. Les Dallys, as equilibrists, and Roxea Loyal, the juggler, are competent performers, and there are others, too numerous to mention, who will communicate to many that old authentic pulse-beat of the ring.

As for the animals, which account for one-third of the items in the show, the forest-bred lions behave themselves regally under duress, and the horses cut noble figures at the crack of the whip. Against a not-sufficiently subdued background of noise from the innumerable side-shows the voice of the ring-master and the jokes of the clowns sometimes lose themselves in the spacious ring, but that is perhaps a good fault. At least, the circus has not yet taken to the microphone!

STUDENTS' CARNIVAL RAISES £3,000

At a meeting of the Board of Management of the Birmingham United Hospital, held at the Queen's Hospital on Friday, representatives of the Birmingham University students handed to the Chairman (Lord Austin) a cheque for £3,000 on account of the proceeds of the Hospital Carnival, 1937. This amount will be applied to the dedication of beds at the new hospital at Edgbaston. When the accounts have been completed, it is hoped that the contribution will be considerably increased.

CENTENARY OF A BIRMINGHAM FIRM

A five-day week for factory workers, regular free Saturdays for the office staff, and a full week's pay to all employees are among the concessions it has been decided to make by Alfred Bird and Sons, Birmingham, to celebrate the centenary of a company whose fortunes have been founded largely on the production of custard powder.

Sir Robert Bird, M.P., chairman of the company, announced the concessions at a gathering of workpeople at Devonshire Works. The five-day week in the factory is to be an experiment and, with the concession to the office staff, was described as "another sign of the constant adaptation of the firm to the demands of 20th Century life." Holidays with pay have been a feature of the organisation for years.

Tennal Grange, Tennal Road, Harborne, 31st December 1937.

A retirement presentation to the General Manager of the Prince of
Wales Theatre, Harry Rushworth (third left), Central Restaurant,
4th January 1938. The diminutive comedian, Wee Georgie Wood
is on the extreme left.

Aston Hall, January 1938.

Yardley Radio Stores, Coventry Road,
Yardley, c. 1938.

The Lord Mayor, Coun Ernest Canning, helps to serve dinners at the Ex-Servicemen's canteen, Windmill Street, 19th January 1938.

Post-Christmas entertainment at the Birmingham Variety Artists' Social Club, Dale End, January 1938.

General Manager, Leslie Holderness, presents the Chief Usherette, Pat Ayres, with the Award of Merit, Paramount, New Street, 1938. The cinema was re-named the Odeon shortly afterwards.

Billy Monk's Orchestra, resident at the West End Ballroom, 1938. They had just been declared winners of the Melody Maker County Dance Band Championship for 1937/38.

Guests at the Annual Dinner of the Circle Francais, Midland Hotel, New Street, 13th March 1938. The Earl of Dudley stands fourth from the left.

Watery Lane, with Woodgate Lane on the left, Quinton, April 1938.

The Kings Norton cinema, The Green, 16th April 1938.

Rednal tram terminus, Summer 1938.

"Primrose Hill", the home of George Cadbury, later Fircroft College, Bristol Road, Selly Oak, 1938.

Staff at Spurrel and Simpson (plating works), Ryland Street, c. 1938.

Gravelly Hill/Tyburn Road, Erdington, 1938.

Jarrett, Rainsford and Laughton Ltd. (hairpin manufacturers), Alexandra Works,
Kent Street/Lower Essex Street, c. 1938.

Bournville Green, 1938.

Boys Brigade band practise, City Road Baptist Church,
Edgbaston, 1938.

High Street/Church Road, Erdington, 1938.

Official Programme July 11ᵀᴴ–16ᵀᴴ 1938.

TWOPENCE

Birmingham 1838-1938 Charter Centenary Celebrations

Centenary Celebrations

1838 - 1938

VISIT OF

THEIR MAJESTIES
THE KING AND QUEEN

THURSDAY, 14th JULY, 1938

• •

Programme

THEIR MAJESTIES THE KING AND QUEEN, attended by the Lady Helen Graham, the Right Hon. Neville Chamberlain, M.P. (Prime Minister), Sir Eric Mièville, K.C.I.E., C.S.I., C.M.G., Lieut.-Col. the Hon. Piers Legh, will arrive by special train at New Street Station (No. 3 platform).

THEIR MAJESTIES will be received at the Station by the Lord Mayor (Councillor E. R. Canning, J.P.).

The Right Hon. Neville Chamberlain, Minister-in-Attendance, will present the Lord Mayor and the High Sheriff of Warwickshire (Mr. Baron Ash) to Their Majesties.

The Lord Lieutenant of Warwickshire (Brig.-General Lord Henry Seymour, D.S.O.) and the Lady Helen Seymour will join the train *en route*.

The Lord Mayor will ask leave to make the following presentations :

    The Lady Mayoress (Mrs. E. R. Canning).
    The Recorder
    The Town Clerk
    The Chief Constable

Miss Joan Canning will have the honour of offering a bouquet to Her Majesty THE QUEEN.

The Lord Mayor and Lady Mayoress, the Recorder and the Town Clerk, will proceed to the Hospitals Centre to await the arrival of the Royal cars.

L OOKING back through the past century one marvels at the progress of this great City of Birmingham. It is to the Citizens, who, in those hundred years, had the foresight to build new factories, create new industries, plan new methods, that we owe our present prosperity. Let us carry on their work, keeping with the times, ever remembering our watchword "Forward."

Public Thanksgiving Service

VICTORIA SQUARE
11th July, 1938, 10-45 a.m.

ORDER OF SERVICE

HYMN - - "Now thank we all our God."

The Reverend Dr. A. Cohen will read from the Scriptures of the Old Testament.
The Very Reverend the Provost of Birmingham will lead the people in an Act of Praise and Thanksgiving.

HYMN - - "Our fathers built this City."

Brigadier C. Newton, Divisional Commander of the Salvation Army will read from the Scriptures of the New Testament.
The Rev. Leyton Richards will lead the people in an Act of Intercession.

HYMN - - "O God of Bethel, by whose hand."

The Rector of Birmingham will lead the people in an Act of Dedication.
The Right Reverend the Lord Bishop of Birmingham will give the BLESSING.

HYMN - - "Rise up, O men of God."

THE CHARTER OF INCORPORATION

The epilogue to the Pageant of Birmingham, part of the centenary celebrations, 11th July 1938.

Preparing to take part in the Pageant Ball at the Palais de Danse, in Monument Road, Edgbaston, "Dr Priestley and his wife" enter their coach, 1938.

The statue to Dr Joseph Priestley, Presbyterian Minister and chemist (his name was given to the Priestley Riots), Chamberlain Square, 1938.

Cottages at the junction of Pool Lane and Queens Road, Yardley, 1938.

Due to the King's illness it was actually opened
by the Duke and Duchess of Gloucester.

Edward Road Baptist Church Young Crusaders Football Team,
Balsall Heath, 1938.

George Dixon School for Girls, City Road, Edgbaston, 1938.

Harborne Post Office, shortly after a burglary had taken place, High Street, 13th November 1938.

Examining the air raid siren, after a test, General Electric Co. Ltd.,
Electric Avenue, Witton, November 1938.

Peace in our time, but not for long, High Street, December 1938.

Hilda Burton, winner of the Miss Birmingham Competition, flanked by the runners-up, Grand Casino ballroom, Corporation Street, c. 1938.

The Pavilion cinema, Pershore Road, Stirchley, 1938.

Colmore Row, 27th December 1938.

Police Ball, Palais de Danse, Monument Road, Edgbaston, c. 1938.

The Birmingham Branch of the British Magical Society's Annual Dinner, West End Ballroom, 1939.

The King and Lord Dudley visit the British Industries Fair, Castle Bromwich, 1st March 1939.

The King and Queen visit Cadbury's, 1st March 1939.

The Queen, accompanied by Viscountess Halifax, arrives at Joseph Lucas Ltd., Great King Street, Hockley, 1st March 1939.

Delightful Motor Runs from Birmingham.

ROUTE FOUR.   Distance 118 miles.

BIRMINGHAM.   By Route No. 5 to (17) KIDDERMINSTER. Leave by Bewdley Rd. for *Wribbenhall*. (3) *Bewdley*. (3½) A.A. BOX (*Callow Hill*). (2½) *Clows Top*. (1¾) *Mamble*. (3½) *Newnham*. (3½) TENBURY. *Burford*. (3) *Little Hereford*. (2½) A.A. BOX (*Woofferton*). (¾) *Brimfield*. (2¼) *Ashton*. (4½) LEOMINSTER. (4) A.A. BOX (*Hope-under-Dinmore*). (3¾) *Wellington Marsh*. *Holmer*. (5) HEREFORD. (2) *Tupsley*. *Lugwardine*. (2) *Hagley*. (4) *Tarrington*. (7) LEDBURY. (1¼) A.A. BOX (*Tewkesbury Turn*). (3¼) *Wynds Point* (*British Camp*). (3¾) GREAT MALVERN. (1½) *Malvern Link*. (4) *Powick*. (2½) WORCESTER. (3½) *Fernhill Heath*. *Martin Hussingtree*. (3¼) DROITWICH.   Straight on, joining the return of Route No. 5 to (19¾) BIRMINGHAM.

JOSEPH LUCAS LIMITED

TELEGRAMS & CABLES.
"LUCAS, BIRMINGHAM"

TELEPHONES:
NORTHERN 5201 (12 LINES)

MANAGING DIRECTORS' OFFICE

HEAD OFFICES
GREAT KING ST.
BIRMINGHAM, 19

YOUR REF.
OUR REF. OL/JAP

13th March 1939

Dear Mr. Pacy,

My Mother has asked me to say how very deeply she appreciates the kindly thought and deep regard which has inspired the various members of the organisation who have approached you with a request to pay some last tribute to "the Guvnor".

I feel that some explanation of his viewpoint will help those interested to realise that it was no mere whim when he specified "no flowers", as he was one of the very earliest and staunchest advocates of funeral reform, having seen so many examples where money which could be ill afforded was spent on a display of last rites.

You know my father was, a man of strong views and Mother and I feel it is the least we can do now that he has gone, to set an example in the present instance, but the gesture which has just been conveyed to us, viz. that a tribute of flowers should be sent to the Hospitals we think will be a means of bringing joy to the sick and we are sure would not run contrary to his views.

On behalf of my Mother, therefore, I would like to accept the suggestion in a deeply heartfelt manner.

With kindest personal regards,

Yours sincerely,

Oliver Lucas

S. Arrol Pacy, Esq.

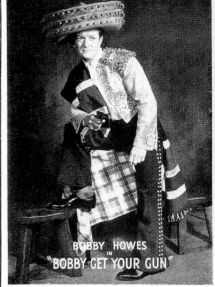

Edmund Fisher enrols in the 48th Division Signals, Cateswell House, Cateswell Road, Hall Green, 18th April 1939.

Warwick Road, Acocks Green, 1939.

Guests arriving at the meeting of the Women's Voluntary Services,
Town Hall, 25th April 1939.

The new Civic Centre, at the rear of the Hall of Memory, under construction, 23rd May 1939.
It later became Baskerville House.

Public Wash House, St George's Street, 1939.

High Street, 28th June 1939.

Cadbury's Works Silver Band, Rowheath Pavilion,
Bournville, c. 1939.

Modelling Latex swimwear designed and manufactured at
Dunlop Rubber Co. Ltd, Erdington, 1939.

In a downpour of rain, which persisted for hours and virtually ruined weeks of careful planning, the Duchess of Kent opened Birmingham Airport on Saturday afternoon. Instead of the expected crowd of between fifty and a hundred thousand spectators, not more than about ten thousand people were present to hear her declare the airport open and to watch the curtailed aviation display given by units of the Royal Air Force and Fleet Air Arm.

Despite the rain, the Duchess, once well described as "the smiling princess," looked happy enough, and was among the first to sympathise with Alderman A. H. James, Chairman of the Airport Committee, for such a depressing climax to many years of hard work. She was received by Alderman James at the entrance to the terminal buildings and presented to various officials before unveiling a plaque commemorating the occasion.

The crowds just after the opening of Elmdon Airport, 8th July 1939.

A typical thirties publicity photograph with models posing in front of a Tiger Moth, Elmdon Airport, July 1939.

Blackout preparations at the offices of the Evening Despatch, Newspaper House, Corporation Street, 13th July 1939.

New Street, 14th July 1939.

As part of an air raid precaution's exercise the Town Clerk, Sir Frank Wiltshire (left), plots imaginary bomb damage in the city centre, 9th August 1939.

The telephonist's room, Council House, 9th August 1939.

HITLER SENDS FOR FOUR AMBASSADORS

Missions Leave Moscow

SIR NEVILE HENDERSON, BRITISH AMBASSADOR IN BERLIN, IS FLYING TO LONDON TODAY TO REPORT TO THE FOREIGN SECRETARY ON HIS MEETING YESTERDAY WITH HERR HITLER.

He is not expected to make a long stay in this country, the Foreign Office announced last night.

The Ambassador, like the envoys of France, Italy and Japan, was summoned to the Chancellery yesterday by Herr Hitler. Herr von Ribbentrop was present at the interviews.

Earlier Hitler had resumed his conference with General Brauchitsch and Admiral Raeder, Commanders-in-Chief of the Army and Navy.

A TENSE SCENE IN THE COMMONS

UNITED RESOLVE TO END AGGRESSION

HITLER'S CHALLENGE ACCEPTED

BRITAIN AND FRANCE TO FIGHT IN DEFENCE OF FREEDOM

THE KING'S MESSAGE TO THE EMPIRE

"STAND CALM, FIRM AND UNITED"

"BRITAIN IS AT WAR WITH GERMANY"

In a broadcast from Downing Street, at 11.15 a.m. on Sunday, Sept. 3, 1939, the Prime Minister said :—

"THIS morning the British Ambassador in Berlin handed the German Government a final Note stating that unless we heard from them by eleven o'clock that they were prepared at once to withdraw their troops from Poland a state of war would exist between us.

" I have to tell you now that no such undertaking has been received, and that consequently this country is at war with Germany.

" You can imagine what a bitter blow it is to me that all my long struggle to win peace has failed. Yet I cannot believe that there is anything more, or anything different that I could have done and that would have been more successful.

" Up to the very last it would have been quite possible to have arranged a peaceful and honourable settlement between Germany and Poland, but Hitler would not have it.

" He had evidently made up his mind to attack Poland whatever happened, and although he now says he put forward reasonable proposals which were rejected by the Poles, that is not a true statement.

" The proposals were never shown to the Poles, nor to us, and though they were announced in a German broadcast on Thursday night Hitler did not wait to hear comments on them, but ordered his troops to cross the Polish frontier. His action shows convincingly that there is no chance of expecting that this man will ever give up his practice of using force to gain his will. He can only be stopped by force.

" We and France are today, in fulfilment of our obligations, going to the aid of Poland, who is so bravely resisting this wicked and unprovoked attack on her people.

" We have a clear conscience. We have done all that any country could do to establish peace.

" The situation in which no word given by Germany's ruler could be trusted and no people or country could feel themselves safe has become intolerable.

" And now that we have resolved to finish it I know that you will all play your part with calmness and courage.

" At such a moment as this the assurances of support that we have received from the Empire are a source of profound encouragement to us.

" When I have finished speaking certain detailed announcements will be made on behalf of the Government. Give these your closest attention.

" The Government have made plans under which it will be possible to carry on the work of the nation in the days of stress and strain that may be ahead. But these plans need your help.

" You may be taking your part in the fighting services or as a volunteer in one of the branches of civil defence. If so, you will report for duty in accordance with the instructions you have received.

" You may be engaged in work essential to the prosecution of war, for the maintenance of the life of the people—in factories, in transport, in public utility concerns, or in the supply of other necessaries of life.

" If so, it is of vital importance that you should carry on with your jobs.

" Now may God bless you all. May He defend the right. It is the evil things that we shall be fighting against—brute force, bad faith, injustice, oppression and persecution—and against them I am certain that the right will prevail."

Children try out their gas masks, 1939.

If Hitler uses Blister gas

Soap and Water will help to beat him

People who are splashed by a blister gas bomb and do not take off any splashed clothing and have treatment AT ONCE may develop bad burns. THE NATION CAN'T AFFORD TO HAVE MEN·OR WOMEN OFF WORK EVEN FOR A SHORT TIME BECAUSE OF GAS BURNS.

There will be no need to be alarmed if you know what to do.

The two best known kinds of blister gas are oily liquids—Mustard, which smells something like onions or garlic, and Lewisite which smells of geraniums. Your gas mask will protect such vital parts of your body as your eyes and lungs. So have it always handy, even when in bed.

WHAT YOU NEED FOR TREATMENT

Anti-Gas Ointment No. 2 or **Bleach Cream** to deal with actual splashes on the skin.

Soap and water, preferably warm, to wash the whole body so as to remove any gas which may have reached the skin either directly or through the clothing.

WHAT YOU SHOULD DO

NOW. Buy the Ointment from your chemist (it only costs a few pence) and keep it with your gas mask, together with a piece of clean rag. If there are gas attacks chemists will have a pail of Bleach Cream outside their shops. But you may be some distance from a chemist's shop and ought to have the Ointment with you.

CITY OF BIRMINGHAM

All Communications must be addressed to the Department and not to Individuals

AIR RAID PRECAUTIONS DEPARTMENT

19 BROAD STREET

BIRMINGHAM 1

Your reference A.R.P.O.
In your reply M.EB.
please quote

Telephone: MIDland 6026-7-8-9
Telegram: "AIRPRED," BIRMINGHAM

13th September, 1939.

Air Raid Wardens' Service.

Dear Sir/Madam,

I have to inform you that a series of eight lectures, comprising four anti-gas and four first-aid, will be given to volunteers for the above service at 11, Cambridge Street (behind the Hall of Memory) on the following dates:

Tuesday Sept.	26th	-	7.30.p.m.
Thursday "	28th	-	"
Tuesday Oct.	3rd	-	"
Thursday "	5th	-	"
Tuesday "	10th	-	"
Thursday "	12th	-	"
Tuesday "	17th	-	"
Thursday "	19th	-	"

Will you please do your utmost to take this course and let me have your reply on the enclosed prepaid postcard.

Yours faithfully,

Victor J. Hamilton

Air Raid Precautions Officer.

Evacuation begins, 1939.

The Grove cinema, Dudley Road, 1939.

A selection of the gas masks that had been left on city transport, Central Lost Property Office, Miller Street, 20th September 1939.

The Lord Mayor, Ald. Theodore Pritchett, takes part in a filmed wartime appeal, Council House, November 1939.

The King arrives, in uniform, on one of his frequent morale-building visits to the city, 26th October 1939.

Town Clerk, Sir Frank Wiltshire, the Lord Mayor, Ald. Theodore Pritchett and Canon Guy Rogers, at the Civic Service, St Martin's, 12th November 1939.

Derek Salberg entertains the younger members of the "Jack and the Beanstalk" cast, The Alexandra Theatre, December 1939.

Two of the principals of the Alexandra Theatre's "Jack and the Beanstalk", husband and wife team, Shaun Glenville and Dorothy Ward, go through their sheet music, Midland Hotel, 11th December 1939. She was the daughter of a Birmingham publican.

Back Cover: The coolest place to visit on the first day of the school holidays, Chamberlain Square, 31st July 1939.

ACKNOWLEDGEMENTS

(for providing photographs, for encouragement and numerous other favours)

Norman and Gloria Bailey; Claude Bevan; The Birmingham City Council Dept. of Planning and Architecture; The Birmingham International Airport; The Birmingham Post and Mail Ltd.; Nell Blackburn; Lorraine Boyce; Carole Burton; Dave and Kath Carpenter; David and Dorothy Fleming; Mike Gancia; Hazel Godwin; Doug Hobson; Anne Jennings; Dave, Thelma and Tom Jones; Thelma Jones; Joyce Lockwood; Dr Ian McWhirter; Brenda Middleton; Dennis Moore; George Peace; David Perrins; Victor J. Price; Clyde Riley; Bill and Peter Samuels; Keith Shakespeare; Joan Wanty; Rosemary Wilkes; Albert Williams; Ken Windsor.

Please forgive any possible omissions. Every effort has been made to include all organisations and individuals involved in the book.

Warwickshire Yeomanry at summer camp, 1938.